PHONEMIC AWARENESS FOR KIDS WITH DYSLEXIA

Workbook with 100 Activities to improve reading skills in kids with dyslexia, aphasia and struggling readers.

Volume 1

GoodWritings

TABLE OF CONTENTS

Beginning Alphabet A–Z 1-26

Beginning Letters... 27-34

I Can Spell 35-42

Rainbow Syllables... 43-50

Counting Syllables... 51-58

Phonemic Counting... 59-66

Vowels... 67-74

Short Vowels 75-79

Long Vowels... 80-84

CVC Words... 85-92

I Can Read Words... 93-100

TABLE OF CONTENTS

Beginning Alphabet A–Z 1-26

Beginning Letters 27-34

I Can Spell 35-42

Rainbow Syllables 43-50

Counting Syllables 51-58

Phonemic Counting 59-66

Vowels 67-74

Short Vowels 75-79

Long Vowels 80-84

CVC Words 85-92

I Can Read Words 93-100

INTRODUCTION

How to Improve Phonemic Awareness in Kids:

Phonemic awareness is the ability to hear, recognize and manipulate sounds in spoken words. It is an essential skill for literacy development in kids, as it helps them learn how to read and write. If you're a parent or educator looking to enhance the phonemic awareness of the children in your care, here are some tips to consider:

1. Play games with sounds
   - Playing games and activities which highlight sounds is a fun, yet effective way to improve phonemic awareness. For example, you could play a game where children identify the initial sound in a word, or match pictures that rhyme.
2. Sing songs and recite rhymes
   - Singing songs and reciting rhymes is an engaging way to help children learn to identify sounds in words. Encourage kids to participate in singing and reciting, and make learning fun.

INTRODUCTION

3. Read regularly with your child

- Reading is one of the best ways to improve phonemic awareness. When reading to your child, emphasize the sounds in words and point them out in the text. You can also play with alliteration and use sound effects.

4. Use visual aids

- Using visual aids, such as pictures or objects, can help children connect sounds with symbols. For instance, you could use cards with pictures of objects and ask children to match them with the corresponding sounds.

5. Practice phonics

- Phonics is the relationship between sounds and the letters that represent them. Teaching children phonics can improve their phonemic awareness and help them read and write. Use games and activities to help children learn phonics, such as matching letters with sounds or creating sound word families.

INTRODUCTION

In conclusion, improving phonemic awareness is an essential part of literacy development in kids, and it can be fun and engaging with the right tools and techniques. Incorporate these tips into your daily routine, and watch as children develop their phonemic awareness and grow into confident readers and writers.

Aa

Say the name of each picture. Tick the box if the picture begins with letter "Aa".

Bb

Say the name of each picture. Tick the box if the picture begins with letter "Bb".

Cc

Say the name of each picture. Tick the box if the picture begins with letter "Cc".

Dd

Say the name of each picture. Tick the box if the picture begins with letter "Dd".

Ee

Say the name of each picture. Tick the box if the picture begins with letter "Ee".

Ff

Say the name of each picture. Tick the box if the picture begins with letter "Ff".

Gg

Say the name of each picture. Tick the box if the picture begins with letter "Gg".

☐

☐

☐

☐

☐

☐

☐

Hh

Say the name of each picture. Tick the box if the picture begins with letter "Hh".

Ii

Say the name of each picture. Tick the box if the picture begins with letter "Ii".

Jj

Say the name of each picture. Tick the box if the picture begins with letter "Jj".

Kk

Say the name of each picture. Tick the box if the picture begins with letter "Kk".

Ll

Say the name of each picture. Tick the box if the picture begins with letter "Ll".

Mm

Say the name of each picture. Tick the box if the picture begins with letter "Mm".

Nn

Say the name of each picture. Tick the box if the picture begins with letter "Nn".

Oo

Say the name of each picture. Tick the box if the picture begins with letter "Oo".

☐ (otter)

☐ (snake)

☐ (owl)

☐ (turtle)

☐ (orange)

☐ (octopus)

☐ (ostrich)

Pp

Say the name of each picture. Tick the box if the picture begins with letter "Pp".

Qq

Say the name of each picture. Tick the box if the picture begins with letter "Qq".

☐

☐

☐

☐

☐

☐

☐

☐

Rr

Say the name of each picture. Tick the box if the picture begins with letter "Rr".

Ss

Say the name of each picture. Tick the box if the picture begins with letter "Ss".

☐ (ball)

☐ (socks)

☐ (sun)

☐ (star)

☐ (strawberries)

☐ (bee)

☐ (snail)

Tt

Say the name of each picture. Tick the box if the picture begins with letter "Tt".

Uu

21

V v

Say the name of each picture. Tick the box if the picture begins with letter "Vv".

☐

☐

☐

☐

☐

☐

☐

☐

Ww

Say the name of each picture. Tick the box if the picture begins with letter "Ww".

Xx

Say the name of each picture. Tick the box if the picture begins with letter "Xx".

Yy

Say the name of each picture. Tick the box if the picture begins with letter "Yy".

Zz

Say the name of each picture. Tick the box if the picture begins with letter "Zz".

☐

☐

☐

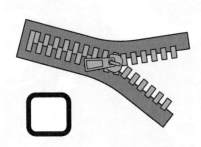

☐

☐

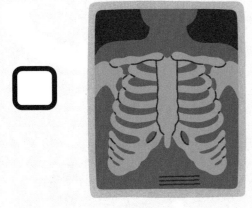

☐

☐

BEGINNING LETTERS

Match each word with the letter that is missing and write it in the blank.

 ☐ ell   •   • **t**

 ☐ ell   •   • **b**

 ☐ all   •   • **y**

 ☐ all   •   • **c**

 ☐ all   •   • **b**

BEGINNING LETTERS

Match each word with the letter that is missing and write it in the blank.

 ☐at • • $\left(\text{s}\right)$

 ☐at • • $\left(\text{r}\right)$

 ☐at • • $\left(\text{c}\right)$

 ☐at • • $\left(\text{b}\right)$

 ☐at • • $\left(\text{m}\right)$

28

BEGINNING LETTERS

Match each word with the letter that is missing and write it in the blank.

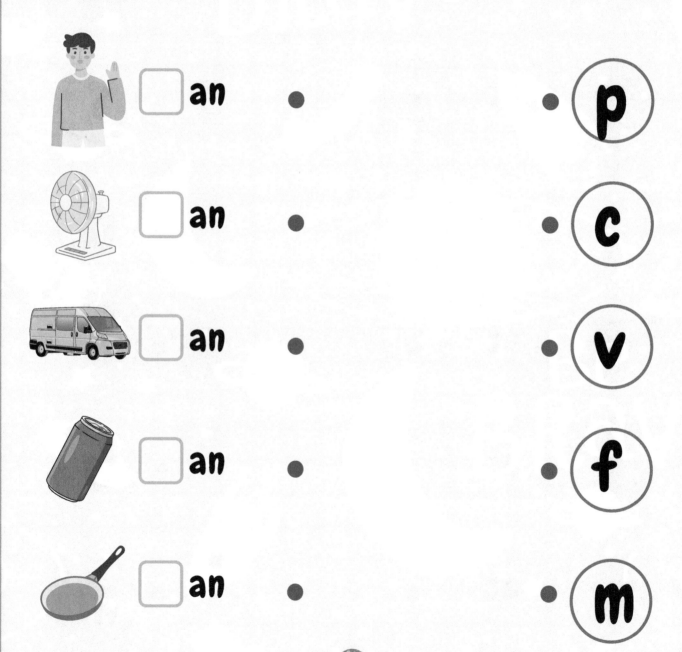

[ ]an • • p

[ ]an • • c

[ ]an • • v

[ ]an • • f

[ ]an • • m

BEGINNING LETTERS

Match each word with the letter that is missing and write it in the blank.

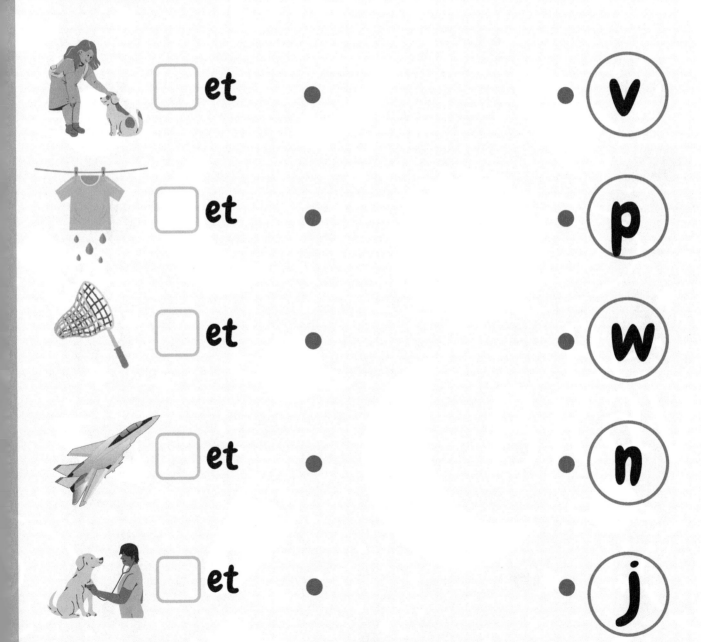

☐et •   • v

☐et •   • p

☐et •   • w

☐et •   • n

☐et •   • j

30

BEGINNING LETTERS

Match each word with the letter that is missing and write it in the blank.

☐ ip   •   • **z**

☐ ip   •   • **d**

☐ ip   •   • **l**

☐ ip   •   • **s**

☐ ip   •   • **h**

BEGINNING LETTERS

Match each word with the letter that is missing and write it in the blank.

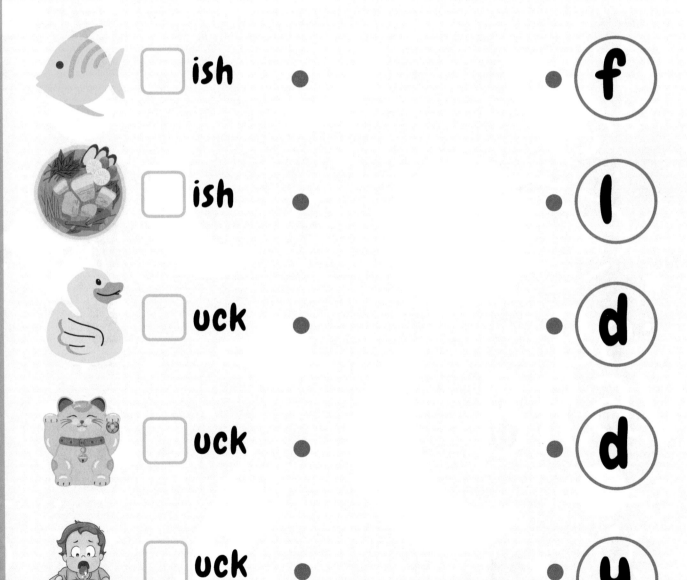

☐ish •   • f

☐ish •   • l

☐uck •   • d

☐uck •   • d

☐uck •   • y

BEGINNING LETTERS

Match each word with the letter that is missing and write it in the blank.

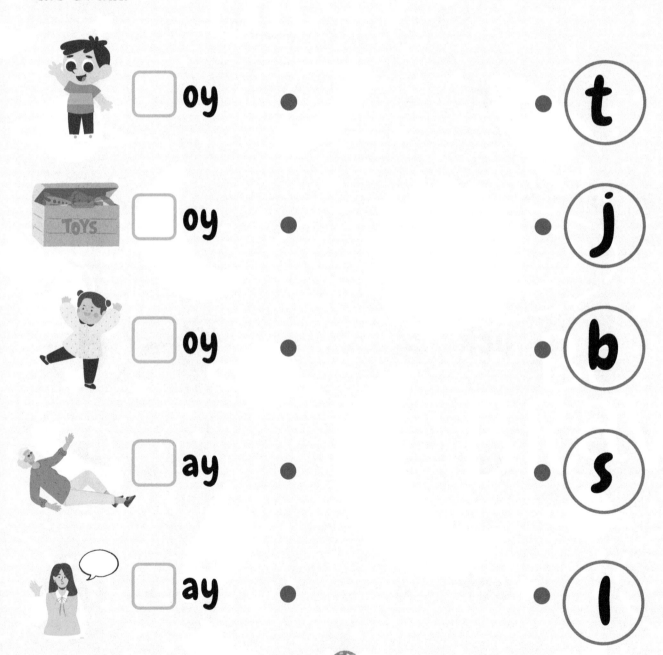

☐ oy • • **t**

☐ oy • • **j**

☐ oy • • **b**

☐ ay • • **s**

☐ ay • • **l**

BEGINNING LETTERS

Match each word with the letter that is missing and write it in the blank.

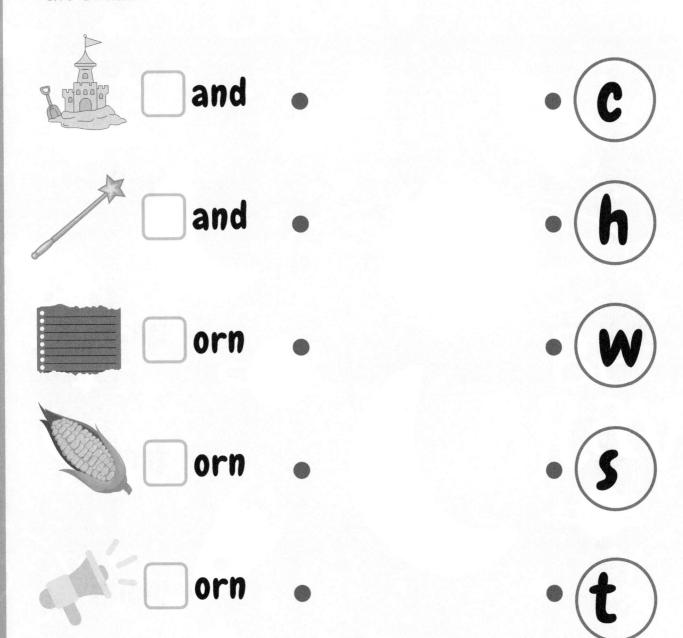

☐ and •

☐ and •

☐ orn •

☐ orn •

☐ orn •

• c

• h

• w

• s

• t

I CAN SPELL

Match the picture to the word.

 •   • bird

 •   • bell

 •   • bear

 •   • tree

 •   • moon

I CAN SPELL

Match the picture to the word.

 •

• **beach**

 •

• **bread**

 •

• **house**

 •

• **heart**

 •

• **horse**

I CAN SPELL

Match the picture to the word.

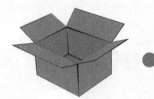 •

• **egg**

 •

• **fox**

 •

• **nut**

 •

• **box**

 •

• **jog**

I CAN SPELL

Match the picture to the word.

 •

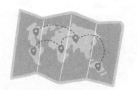 •

• Zip

• Net

 •

• Map

 •

• Toe

 •

• Owl

Match the picture to the word.

 •

 •

 •

 •

 •

• **paw**

• **hen**

• **run**

• **jam**

• **key**

I CAN SPELL

Match the picture to the word.

 •

 •

 •

 •

 •

• **hat**

• **bat**

• **bus**

• **cat**

• **fan**

I CAN SPELL

Match the picture to the word.

 •

• **earth**

 •

• **snow**

 •

• **sand**

 •

• **lock**

 •

• **gift**

I CAN SPELL

Match the picture to the word.

 •

• spoon

 •

• fork

 •

• cake

 •

• drum

 •

• kite

42

DRAW A RAINBOW SYLLABLES

Read the words. Count the syllables. Draw a rainbow line for each syllable.

door

window

chair

refrigerator

DRAW A RAINBOW
SYLLABLES

Read the words. Count the syllables. Draw a rainbow line for each syllable.

cake

apple pie

ice cream

candy

DRAW A RAINBOW
SYLLABLES

Read the words. Count the syllables. Draw a rainbow line for each syllable.

carrot

broccoli

potato

tomato

DRAW A RAINBOW
SYLLABLES

Read the words. Count the syllables. Draw a rainbow line for each syllable.

basketball

tennis

roller skating

swimming

DRAW A RAINBOW
SYLLABLES

Read the words. Count the syllables. Draw a rainbow line for each syllable.

crocodile

alligator

caterpillar

eagle

DRAW A RAINBOW
SYLLABLES

Read the words. Count the syllables. Draw a rainbow line for each syllable.

koala

cinema

policeman

dragonfly

DRAW A RAINBOW
SYLLABLES

Read the words. Count the syllables. Draw a rainbow line for each syllable.

Monday   **Wednesday**

Saturday   **Sunday**

DRAW A RAINBOW
SYLLABLES

Read the words. Count the syllables. Draw a rainbow line for each syllable.

firefly

orange

banana

watermelon

COUNTING SYLLABLES

Read and trace the words. Count how many syllables are in each word and color the numbered box that matches the answer.

papaya

1 2 3 4

strawberry

1 2 3 4

watermelon

1 2 3 4

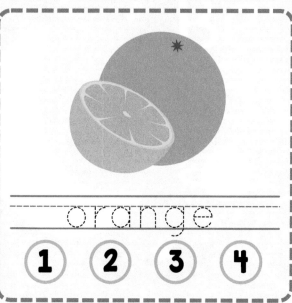

orange

1 2 3 4

COUNTING SYLLABLES

Read and trace the words. Count how many syllables are in each word and color the numbered box that matches the answer.

rabbit

(1) (2) (3) (4)

crocodile

(1) (2) (3) (4)

owl

(1) (2) (3) (4)

eagle

(1) (2) (3) (4)

COUNTING SYLLABLES

Read and trace the words. Count how many syllables are in each word and color the numbered box that matches the answer.

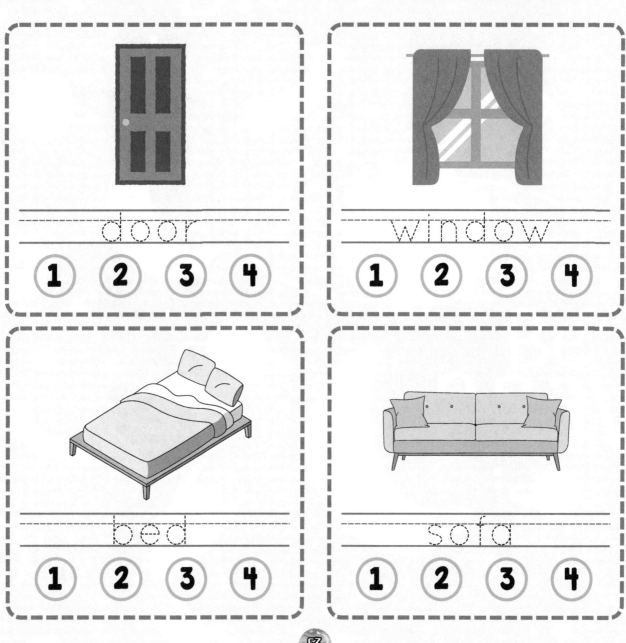

door
1 2 3 4

window
1 2 3 4

bed
1 2 3 4

sofa
1 2 3 4

COUNTING SYLLABLES

Read and trace the words. Count how many syllables are in each word and color the numbered box that matches the answer.

earth

① ② ③ ④

mercury

① ② ③ ④

jupiter

① ② ③ ④

saturn

① ② ③ ④

COUNTING SYLLABLES

Read and trace the words. Count how many syllables are in each word and color the numbered box that matches the answer.

sun

① 1 ② 2 ③ 3 ④ 4

moon

① 1 ② 2 ③ 3 ④ 4

comet

① 1 ② 2 ③ 3 ④ 4

rocketship

① 1 ② 2 ③ 3 ④ 4

COUNTING SYLLABLES

Read and trace the words. Count how many syllables are in each word and color the numbered box that matches the answer.

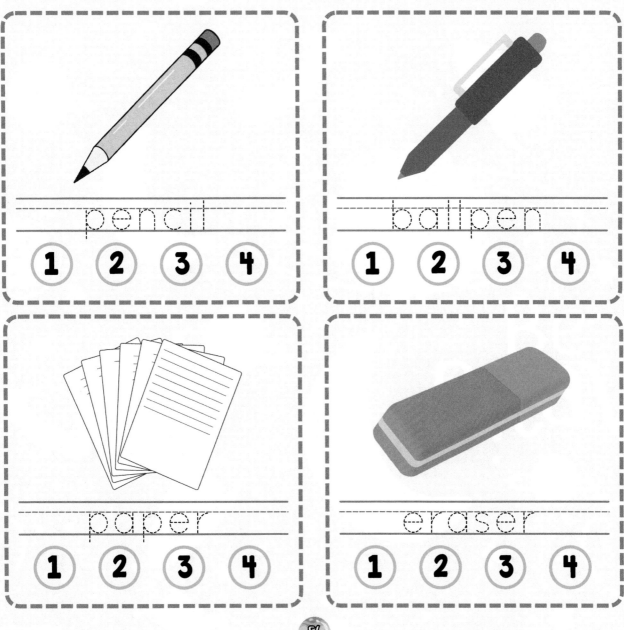

pencil

① 1 ② 2 ③ 3 ④ 4

ballpen

① 1 ② 2 ③ 3 ④ 4

paper

① 1 ② 2 ③ 3 ④ 4

eraser

① 1 ② 2 ③ 3 ④ 4

COUNTING SYLLABLES

Read and trace the words. Count how many syllables are in each word and color the numbered box that matches the answer.

spoon

(1) (2) (3) (4)

sandwich

(1) (2) (3) (4)

chicken

(1) (2) (3) (4)

tomato soup

(1) (2) (3) (4)

COUNTING SYLLABLES

Read and trace the words. Count how many syllables are in each word and color the numbered box that matches the answer.

basketball

1 2 3 4

ice skating

1 2 3 4

volleyball

1 2 3 4

baseball

1 2 3 4

PHONEMES COUNTING

Look at each picture. Say its name. Write the number of phonemes/sound in it.

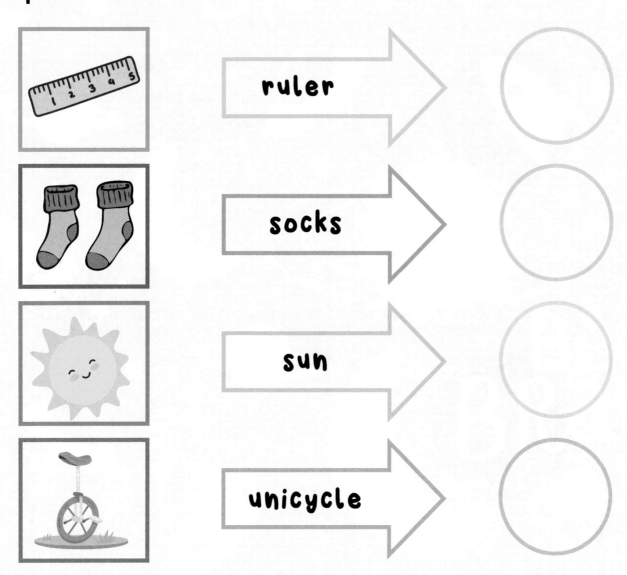

ruler

socks

sun

unicycle

PHONEMES COUNTING

Look at each picture. Say its name. Write the number of phonemes/sound in it.

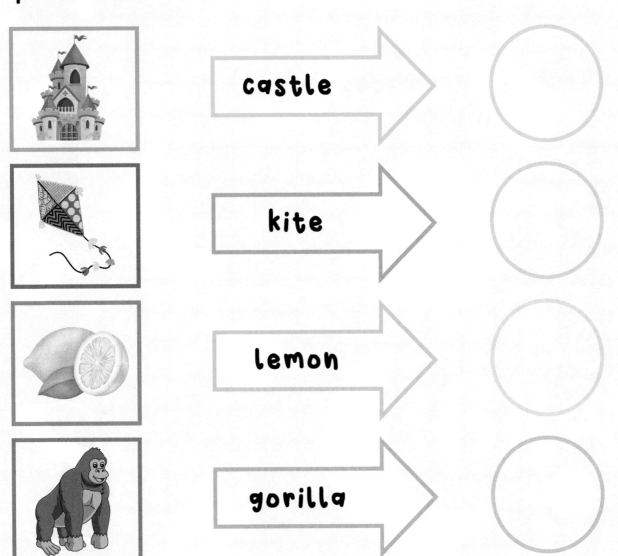

castle

kite

lemon

gorilla

PHONEMES COUNTING

Look at each picture. Say its name. Write the number of phonemes/sound in it.

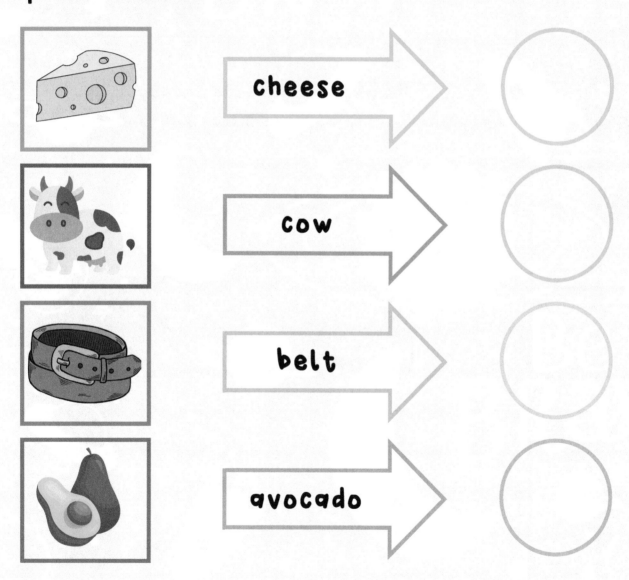

cheese

cow

belt

avocado

PHONEMES COUNTING

Look at each picture. Say its name. Write the number of phonemes/sound in it.

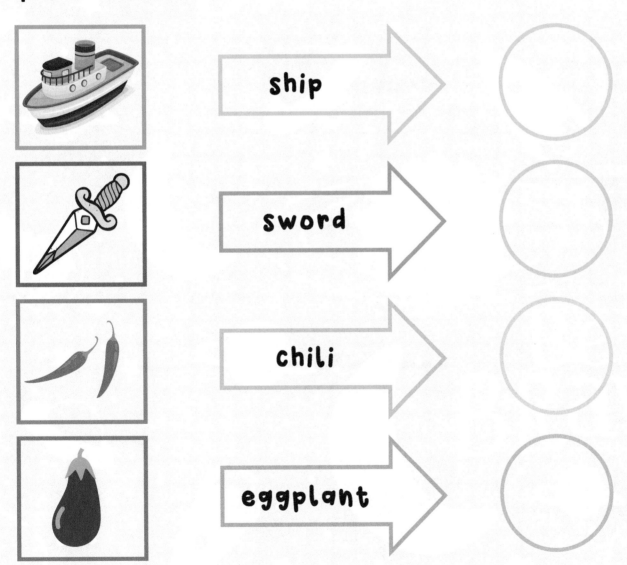

ship →

sword →

chili →

eggplant →

PHONEMES COUNTING

Look at each picture. Say its name. Write the number of phonemes/sound in it.

cookies

lollipop

sand castle

pumpkin

PHONEMES COUNTING

Look at each picture. Say its name. Write the number of phonemes/sound in it.

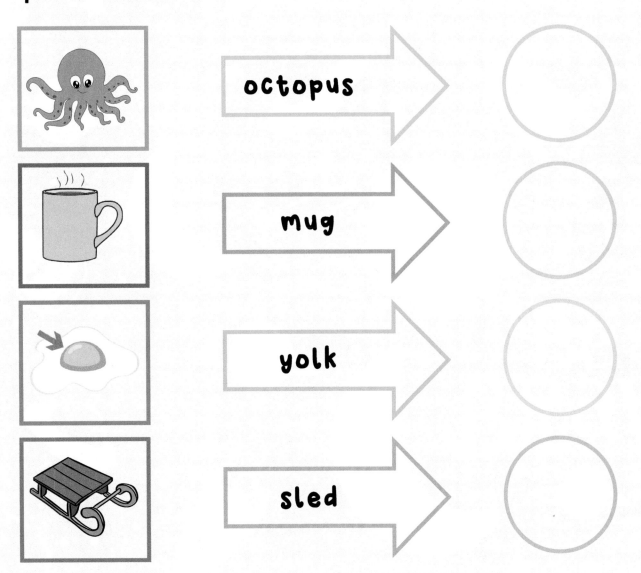

octopus

mug

yolk

sled

PHONEMES COUNTING

Look at each picture. Say its name. Write the number of phonemes/sound in it.

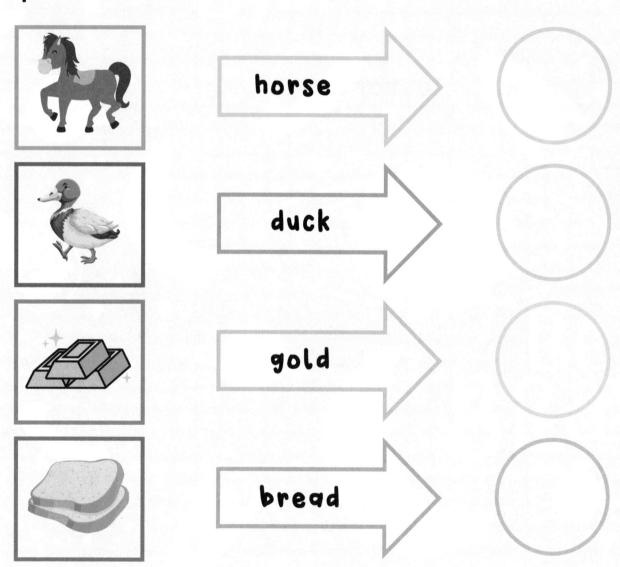

horse →

duck →

gold →

bread →

PHONEMES COUNTING

Look at each picture. Say its name. Write the number of phonemes/sound in it.

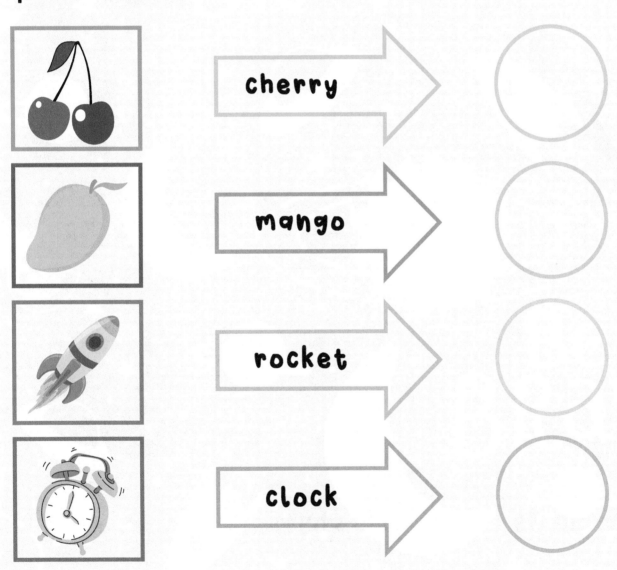

cherry →

mango →

rocket →

clock →

VOWELS

Fill in the missing vowels.

p_n

b_lb

cr_y_ns

p_nc_ls

tr_phy

fr_g

VOWELS

Fill in the missing vowels.

cr_b

d__r

gr_p_s

d_ck

sq__rr_l

_r_n

VOWELS

Fill in the missing vowels.

_g__n_

ch__r

t__

sp__n

r_ng

dr_ss

VOWELS

Fill in the missing vowels.

sh_ _s

sn_ _l

b_rn

d_c_

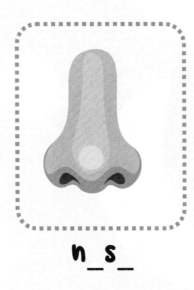

n_s_

b_n_n_

VOWELS

Fill in the missing vowels.

f _ r _

m _ _ th

br _ _ n

m _ n _ y

l _ k _

j _ lly

VOWELS

Fill in the missing vowels.

sn_k_

l_dd_r

_mbr_ll_

v_lt_r_

__l

br_sh

12

VOWELS

Fill in the missing vowels.

b_cycl_

y_y_

p_ng__n

g_ng_r

s_f_

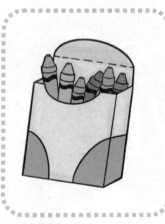

cr_y_ns

VOWELS

Fill in the missing vowels.

wh _ l _

_ sl _ nd

g _ rl _ c

h _ l _ c _ pt _ r

gl _ b _

gr _ p _ s

SHORT VOWELS

Read the word, then circle the picture that matches the word.

FLAG

SAX

BANK

SAD

MAP

SHORT VOWELS

Read the word, then circle the picture that matches the word.

SHELL

HEN

CENT

GEM

BED

SHORT VOWELS

Read the word, then circle the picture that matches the word.

BIN

CHIP

BIB

WIG

LID

SHORT VOWELS

Read the word, then circle the picture that matches the word.

DOG

KNOB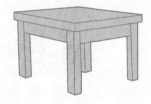

FROG

POD

POT

SHORT VOWELS

Read the word, then circle the picture that matches the word.

SUN

CUB

BUS

BUN

NUT

LONG VOWELS

Read the word, then circle the picture that matches the word.

CAKE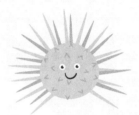

PLATE

HAY

RAIN

SNAKE

LONG VOWELS

Read the word, then circle the picture that matches the word.

SHEEP

CHEESE

LEAF

TEETH

TEA

LONG VOWELS

Read the word, then circle the picture that matches the word.

TIE

PIE

ICE

ICE

KITE

FIVE

LONG VOWELS

Read the word, then circle the picture that matches the word.

CONE

TOMATO

ROBOT

PIANO

BOAT

LONG VOWELS

Read the word, then circle the picture that matches the word.

UNICORN

FRUITS

TISSUE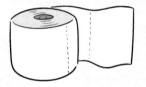

GLUE

RULER

CVC WORDS

Write the correct word in the blank.

cow	cat	pig	jam

 This is a _____.

 This is a _____.

 This is a _____.

 This is a _____.

CVC WORDS

Write the correct word in the blank.

| pan | pen | cap | van |

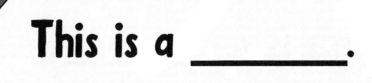

This is a _____.

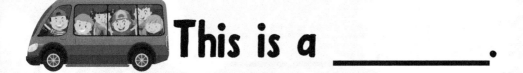

This is a _____.

This is a _____.

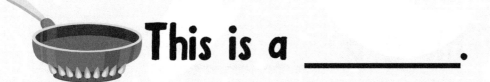

This is a _____.

CVC WORDS

Write the correct word in the blank.

| hen | mat | log | pin |

 This is a _____.

 This is a _____.

 This is a _____.

 This is a _____.

CVC WORDS

Write the correct word in the blank.

| wet | fan | jet | tap |

This is a _____.

This is a _____.

This is a _____.

This is _____.

CVC WORDS

Write the correct word in the blank.

| net | peg | dip | rug |

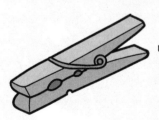 This is a _____.

 This is a _____.

 This is a _____.

 This is a _____.

CVC WORDS

Write the correct word in the blank.

keg	jar	mop	jug

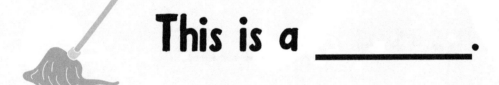

This is a _____.

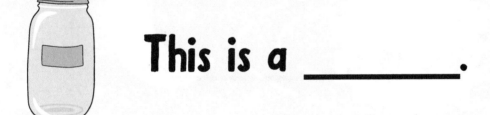

This is a _____.

This is a _____.

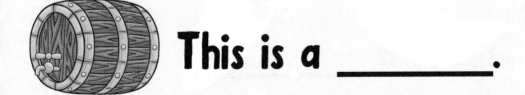

This is a _____.

CVC WORDS

Write the correct word in the blank.

| bus | hat | bat | rod |

This is a _____.

This is a _____.

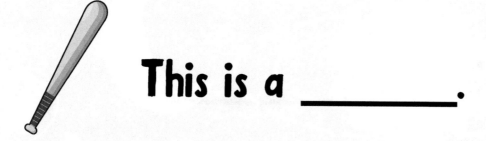

This is a _____.

This is a _____.

CVC WORDS

Write the correct word in the blank.

| dog | lip | tag | bag |

This is a _____.

This is a _____.

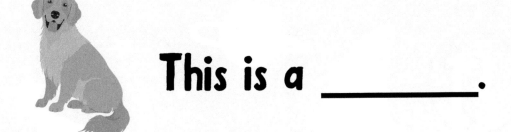
This is a _____.

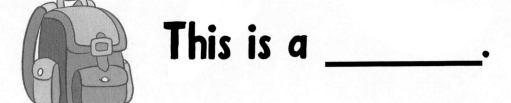
This is a _____.

I CAN READ WORDS

Read the sentence, then color the picture that matches the given word.

I can see a rainbow.

I can see a bird.

I can see a ball.

I can see a snail.

I CAN READ WORDS

Read the sentence, then color the picture that matches the given word.

I can see a dinosaur.

I can see an apple.

I can see a fox.

I can see a bag.

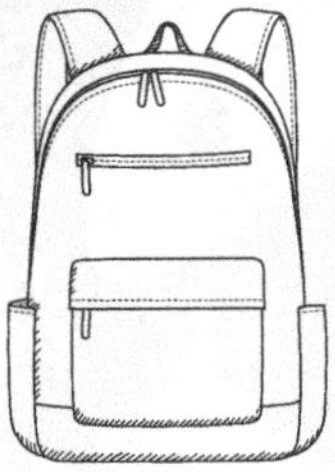

I CAN READ WORDS

Read the sentence, then color the picture that matches the given word.

I can see a zebra.

I can see a strawberry.

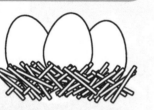  

I can see a crab.

I can see grapes.

I CAN READ WORDS

Read the sentence, then color the picture that matches the given word.

> I can see a lizard.

> I can see a lollipop.

 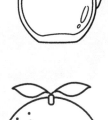 

> I can see a cow.

> I can see a fan.

I CAN READ WORDS

Read the sentence, then color the picture that matches the given word.

I can see a box.

I can see a bin.

I can see a pot.

I can see a dog.

I CAN READ WORDS

Read the sentence, then color the picture that matches the given word.

I can see a clock.

I can see an elephant.

I can see a kid.

I can see a snake.

I CAN READ WORDS

Read the sentence, then color the picture that matches the given word.

I can see a penguin.

I can see a pencil.

I can see a car.

I can see a tree.

I CAN READ WORDS

Read the sentence, then color the picture that matches the given word.

I can see a pair of socks.

I can see a rocket.

I can see a carrot.

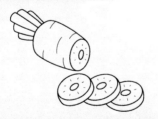  

I can see a corn.

Printed in Great Britain
by Amazon

26665578R00059